3000782

SUPER
SANDCASTLE
Let's Learn A to Z

# Ant Farm
## to
# Zebra Fish

## Pets from A to Z

Mary Elizabeth Salzmann

Consulting Editor, Diane Craig, M.A./Reading Specialist

ABDO
Publishing Company

Published by ABDO Publishing Company, 8000 West 78th Street, Edina, Minnesota 55439. Copyright © 2009 by Abdo Consulting Group, Inc. International copyrights reserved in all countries. No part of this book may be reproduced in any form without written permission from the publisher. Super SandCastle™ is a trademark and logo of ABDO Publishing Company.

Printed in the United States.

Editor: Martha E. H. Rustad
Content Developer: Nancy Tuminelly
Cover and Interior Design and Production: Colleen Dolphin, Mighty Media
Photo Credits: Biosphoto/Klein J.-L. & Hubert M.-L./Peter Arnold Inc., Biosphoto/Tavernier Yvette/Peter Arnold Inc., WILDLIFE/Peter Arnold Inc., Shutterstock

Library of Congress Cataloging-in-Publication Data

Salzmann, Mary Elizabeth, 1968-

   Ant farm to zebra fish : pets from A to Z / Mary Elizabeth Salzmann.

     p. cm. --  (Let's learn A to Z)

   ISBN 978-1-60453-494-8

   1.  Pets--Juvenile literature. 2.  English language--Alphabet--Juvenile literature.  I. Title.

SF416.2.S26 2009

636.088'7--dc22

                    2008023866

Super SandCastle™ books are created by a team of professional educators, reading specialists, and content developers around five essential components—phonemic awareness, phonics, vocabulary, text comprehension, and fluency—to assist young readers as they develop reading skills and strategies and increase their general knowledge. All books are written, reviewed, and leveled for guided reading, early reading intervention, and Accelerated Reader® programs for use in shared, guided, and independent reading and writing activities to support a balanced approach to literacy instruction.

# About Super SandCastle™

## Bigger Books for Emerging Readers
## Grades K-4

Created for library, classroom, and at-home use, Super SandCastle™ books support and engage young readers as they develop and build literacy skills and will increase their general knowledge about the world around them. Super SandCastle™ books are part of SandCastle™, the leading preK–3 imprint for emerging and beginning readers. Super SandCastle™ features a larger trim size for more reading fun.

## Let Us Know

Super SandCastle™ would like to hear your stories about reading this book. What was your favorite page? Was there something hard that you needed help with? Share the ups and downs of learning to read. We want to hear from you! Send us an e-mail.

**sandcastle@abdopublishing.com**

Contact us for a complete list of SandCastle™, Super SandCastle™, and other nonfiction and fiction titles from ABDO Publishing Company.

www.abdopublishing.com • 8000 West 78th Street Edina, MN 55439 • 800-800-1312 • 952-831-1632 fax

This fun and informative series employs illustrated definitions to introduce emerging readers to an alphabet of words in various topic areas. Each page combines words with corresponding images and descriptive sentences to encourage learning and knowledge retention. AlphagalorZ inspires young readers to find out more about the subjects that most interest them!

The "Guess what?" feature expands the reading and learning experience by offering additional information and fascinating facts about specific words or concepts. The "More Words" section provides additional related A to Z vocabulary words that develop and increase reading comprehension.

These books are appropriate for library, classroom, and home use.

# Aa

**Guess what?**

An ant farm is also called a formicarium.

# Ant Farm

People keep pet ants in ant farms. Some ant farms are narrow containers with clear sides. This allows people to see the ants in their tunnels. Ants can also be kept in an aquarium or other glass or plastic container.

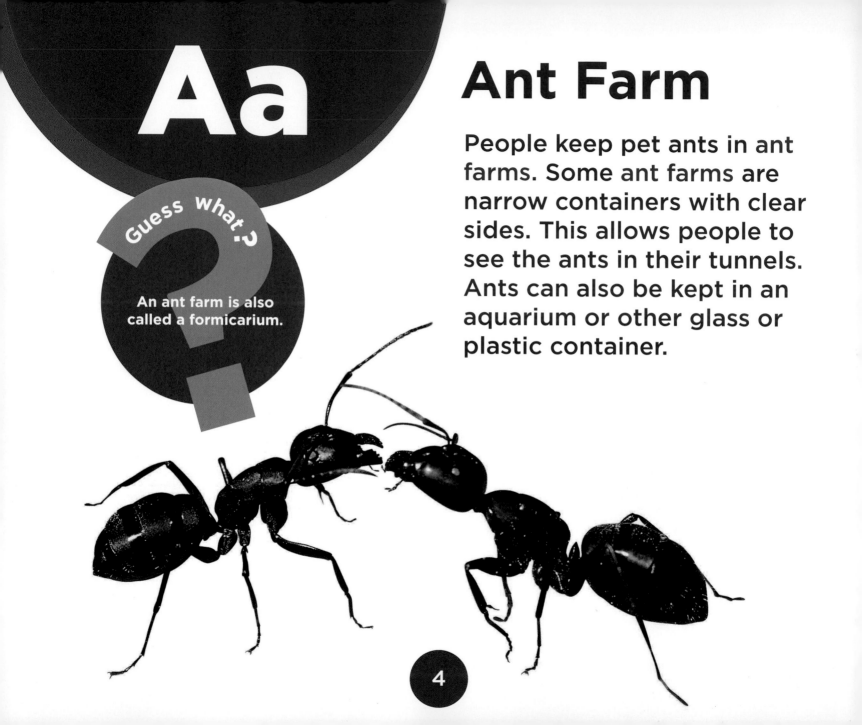

4

## Guess what?

**Budgie** is short for *budgerigar* (BUJ-uh-ree-gar).

# Budgie

A budgie is a kind of parakeet. They are usually green and yellow, but also come in other colors. Budgies are smart and can be taught to say words.

# Cat

Cats have been kept as pets for thousands of years. People like them because they are small, cuddly, and easy to care for. Cats also help keep mice and other pests out of the house.

Cc

# Dog

After cats, dogs are the second most popular pet in the United States. Many dogs are trained to help people. They can herd cattle and sheep, help hunters, and protect homes.

**Guess what?**

There are hundreds of dog breeds.

7

Dd

# Emperor Scorpion

The emperor scorpion can be seven inches (18 cm) long. It is the most common type of pet scorpion. Most emperor scorpion owners don't hold their scorpions because they can sting. The sting is like a bee sting.

**Guess what?**

The emperor scorpion is also called the imperial scorpion.

Ee

# Ferret

**Ff**

Ferrets are popular pets because they are small and playful. They weigh about two pounds (1 kg). Ferrets sleep up to 18 hours a day.

**Guess what?**

Ferrets are related to otters, weasels, and skunks.

9

# Gg

## Guinea Pig

Guinea pigs are larger than most other pet rodents. They learn to recognize their owners and the sounds of their food being prepared. Guinea pigs whistle and chirp loudly when they are excited.

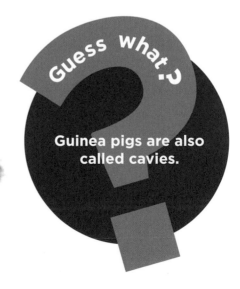

**Guess what?**

Guinea pigs are also called cavies.

# Horse

People keep horses for riding, racing, and working on farms and ranches. There are many breeds of horses, including Arabian, Clydesdale, and quarter horse.

**Guess what?**

Before cars, trains, and airplanes, horses were the main form of transportation.

Arabian stallion

11

# Ii

## Iguana

The iguana is a large lizard. A male iguana can be more than six feet (2 m) long. Iguanas are good climbers, and they can also swim.

**Guess what?**

Keeping an iguana is illegal in some places, including New York City and the state of Hawaii.

# Jackson's Chameleon

Jackson's chameleons are also called three-horned chameleons. This is because the males and some of the females have three horns. They are usually green, but they will turn brown when scared or cold.

Guess what?

**?**

Jackson's chameleons originated in Africa.

13

Jj

# Kinkajou

The kinkajou is related to the raccoon, but it looks and acts a lot like a monkey. Pet kinkajous need to have branches, ledges, and ropes to climb on. Kinkajous are nocturnal and eat fruit.

Guess what?

The kinkajou has a prehensile tail that it uses to climb.

## Kk

**Guess what?**

A baby llama is called a cria.

# Llama

Llamas are usually calm and gentle. They do best if at least two llamas are kept together. Some people use llamas as pack animals, and they can be taught to pull a cart or wagon.

# Mm

Guess what.?

A mouse can fit through an opening smaller than half an inch (1 cm).

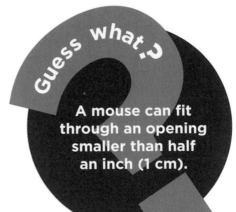

## Mouse

Mice are small rodents that are active and fun to watch. They like to climb and run on exercise wheels. A mouse can be tamed and will learn to take food from its owner's hand.

# Newt

Most newts are semi-aquatic. A newt enclosure needs to have a pool of water deep enough for swimming. It also needs to have a dry land area. Newts eat insects, worms, and snails.

**Guess what?**

Newts look like lizards, but they are amphibians, not reptiles.

**Nn**

# Opossum

The species of opossum most often kept as a pet is the gray short-tailed opossum. They are fairly easy to handle and like to be fed treats. But they will fight with each other, so it is best to keep only one opossum at a time.

**Guess what?**

The gray short-tailed opossum's body is about five inches (13 cm) long. Its tail is almost as long as its body.

Guess what?

Scientists think only humans, primates, dolphins, and whales are smarter than pigs.

# Potbellied Pig

Potbellied pigs are smaller than most other species of pig, but they can still weigh 100 pounds (45 kg) or more. Potbellied pigs can be trained to walk on a leash and use a litter box.

**Pp**

# Qq

# Quaker Parrot

The Quaker parrot is also called the monk parakeet or Quaker parakeet. It originated in South America. The Quaker parrot is one of the easiest parrot species to teach to speak.

**Guess what?**

Quaker parrots are the only kind of parrots that build nests out of sticks. All other parrots live in tree holes.

# Rabbit

Rabbits are popular pets because they are cute, soft, and quiet. They can be trained to use a litter box. Some people take their pet rabbits for walks on leashes.

**Guess what?**

Rabbits are not rodents. They are lagomorphs.

**Rr**

corn snake

# Snake

Three of the most common pet snakes are the ball python, the corn snake, and the king snake. All snakes eat only meat, such as rodents, lizards, and insects. Snakes can't chew their food so they swallow it whole.

**Guess what?**

There are nearly 3,000 species of snakes.

king snake

## Ss

22

ball python

# Tarantula

Tarantulas are large, hairy spiders. Pet tarantulas are kept in glass enclosures called terrariums. Common pet tarantulas are the Chilean rose tarantula and the Mexican redknee tarantula. Tarantulas eat mostly insects.

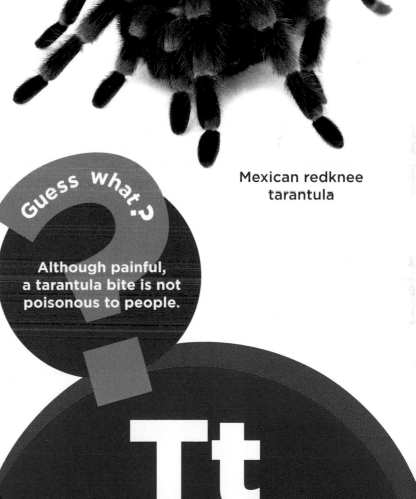

Mexican redknee tarantula

Chilean rose tarantula

**Guess what?**

Although painful, a tarantula bite is not poisonous to people.

Tt

# Upside-Down Catfish

The upside-down catfish was named for its habit of swimming upside-down. It is a good aquarium fish because it's peaceful and fairly small, about four inches (10 cm) long.

**Guess what?**

Upside-down catfish don't swim upside-down until they are about two months old.

**Uu**

# Veterinarian

A veterinarian is a doctor who takes care of animals. People take their pets to a veterinarian for checkups and when they get hurt or sick.

**Guess what?**

Some veterinarians specialize in certain types of animals, such as horses, reptiles, or birds.

# Ww

**Guess what?**

The two species of water dragon are the Chinese water dragon and the Australian water dragon.

Chinese
water dragon

# Water Dragon

Water dragons are large lizards. The males can be three feet (1 m) long, so they need large enclosures. The enclosure needs to have water for them to swim in. Water dragons eat insects, worms, and small fish.

Australian
water dragon

26

# eXotic Pet

An exotic pet is any animal that is rarely kept as a pet and is usually only found in the wild or in zoos. Exotic pets include foxes, skunks, monkeys, alligators, and wild cats. Most exotic pets are expensive and take a lot of time and effort to care for properly.

**Guess what?**

Many places don't allow people to keep certain types of exotic pets.

# Yy

## Yak

The yak originated in Tibet. For hundreds of years, people have used yaks to carry supplies and pull plows. Yak hair can be spun into yarn, and their milk can be made into cheese and yogurt.

**Guess what?**

Yaks are social animals and can learn to come when called.

28

# Zebra Fish

The zebra fish is a very common aquarium fish. It is also called the zebra danio. Zebra fish have blue and silver stripes. They are about one and a half inches (4 cm) long.

Guess what?

Zebra fish lay 300 to 500 eggs at a time.

Zz

# Glossary

breed – a group of animals or plants that have ancestors and characteristics in common.

checkup – a routine examination by a doctor.

container – something that other things can be put into.

cuddly – suitable for being held close.

enclosure – a device such as a cage, tank, or fence used to confine something.

exotic – very different or unusual.

insect – a small creature with two or four wings, six legs, and a body with three sections.

ledge – a narrow flat surface that sticks out from a wall.

male – being of the sex that can father offspring. Fathers are male.

nocturnal – most active at night.

parakeet – a small parrot with brightly colored feathers and a long, pointed tail.

plow – a farm machine used to cut, lift, and turn over soil.

prehensile – able to wrap around and grasp something.

primate – a mammal with developed hands and feet, a large brain, and a short nose, such as a human, ape, or monkey.

ranch – a place where livestock such as cattle, horses, or sheep are raised.

rarely – not very often.

related – having a relationship or connection.

reptile – a cold-blooded animal, such as a snake or turtle, that moves on its belly or on very short legs.

rodent – a mammal with large, sharp front teeth, such as a rat, mouse, or squirrel.

semi-aquatic – living part of the time in water.

species – a group of related living beings.

tame – to teach a wild animal to be gentle and obedient.

terrarium – a clear enclosure for keeping and observing small animals and plants.

transportation – the act of moving people and things.

whistle – to make a sound by blowing through the nose or puckered lips.

worship – to honor or respect as a god or supernatural power.

yogurt – a food made with curdled milk and active cultures.

# More Pets!

## Can you learn about these pets too?

| | | |
|---|---|---|
| alpaca | fish | otter |
| bearded dragon | frog | parakeet |
| boa constrictor | gecko | parrot |
| box turtle | gerbil | piranha |
| brine shrimp | goat | python |
| canary | goldfish | raccoon |
| carp | guppy | rat |
| chameleon | hamster | rooster |
| chicken | hedgehog | salamander |
| chinchilla | hermit crab | scorpion |
| cockatiel | kangaroo | sea monkey |
| cow | lamb | skunk |
| crab | lizard | spider |
| cricket | lovebird | squirrel |
| donkey | macaw | toad |
| dove | meerkat | tortoise |
| duck | mongoose | turkey |
| echidna | monkey | turtle |
| eel | northern leopard frog | veiled chameleon |
| finch | ocelot | wallaby |

Fraser Valley Elementary Media
125 Eastom Av / P.O. Box 128
Fraser, CO 80442/970-726-8033